LAWS
THAT CHANGED
HISTORY

Key
ENVIRONMENTAL
LAWS

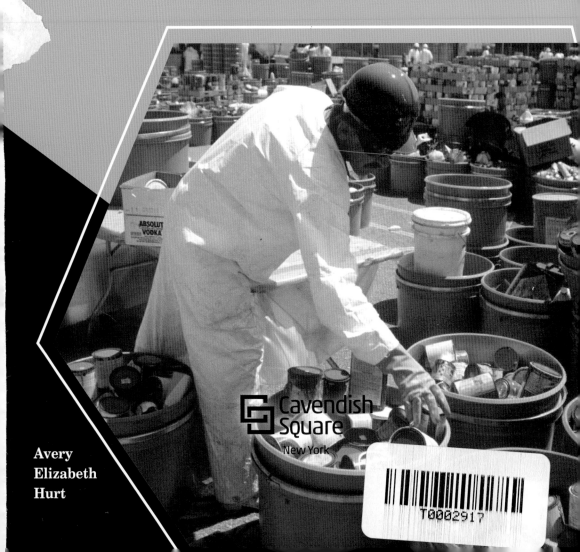

Cavendish
Square
New York

Avery
Elizabeth
Hurt

Published in 2020 by Cavendish Square Publishing, LLC

243 5th Avenue, Suite 136, New York, NY 10016

Copyright © 2020 by Cavendish Square Publishing, LLC

First Edition

Website: cavendishsq.com

This publication represents the opinions and views of the author based on his or her personal experience, knowledge, and research. The information in this book serves as a general guide only. The author and publisher have used their best efforts in preparing this book and disclaim liability rising directly or indirectly from the use and application of this book.

All websites were available and accurate when this book was sent to press.

Library of Congress Cataloging-in-Publication Data

Names: Hurt, Avery Elizabeth.
Title: Key environmental laws / Avery Elizabeth Hurt.
Description: New York : Cavendish Square Publishing, 2020. | Series: Laws that changed history | Includes glossary and index.
Identifiers: ISBN 9781502655233 (pbk.) | ISBN 9781502655240 (library bound) | ISBN 9781502655257 (ebook)
Subjects: LCSH: Environmental law--United States--History--Juvenile literature.
Classification: LCC KF3775.Z9 H84 2020 | DDC 344.7304'6--dc23

Printed in China

Photo Credits: Cover, p. 1 Joseph Sohm/Shutterstock.com; p. 5 Julian Wasser/ The LIFE Images Collection/Getty Images; pp. 8–9 Everett Historical/ Shutterstock.com; p. 11 Alfred Eisenstaedt/The LIFE Images Collection/Getty Images; pp. 12–13 Donna A. Herrmann/Shutterstock.com; p. 16 Sean Pavone/Shutterstock.com; pp. 18–19 Donaldson Collection/Michael Ochs Archives/Getty Images; p. 21 Zhang Peng/LightRocket/Getty Images; p. 23 Narin C/Shutterstock.com; pp. 24–25 The Clay Machine Gun/Shutterstock.com; pp. 28–29 Vladimir Melnik/Shutterstock.com; pp. 32–33 Jean-Louis Atlan/Sygma/Getty Images; pp. 36–37 Michael T Hartman/ Shutterstock.com; pp. 40–41 Lyn Alweis/Denver Post/Getty Images; pp. 42–43 Zack Frank/Shutterstock.com; pp. 44–45 Akkharat Jarusilawong/Shutterstock.com; pp. 48–49 Georgia Evans/Shutterstock.com; pp. 50–51 james_stone76/ Shutterstock.com; p. 53 Nicole S Glass/Shutterstock.com; p. 55 Designua/ Shutterstock.com; pp. 56–57 lassedesignen/Shutterstock.com; p. 61 Rena Schild/ Shutterstock.com; p. 63 d1g1talman/iStock/Getty Images; pp. 64–65 Fedorova Nataliia/Shutterstock.com; p. 67 Alex Wong/Getty Images; Cover, back cover and interior pages Capitol dome graphic Alexkava/Shutterstock.com.

CONTENTS

Introduction

They gathered in schoolyards and city parks. They met on the steps of courthouses and university buildings. They were young and old, rich and poor, Democrats and Republicans. They carried signs that said "Eat Sleep Recycle," "Good Planets Are Hard to Find," and "Love Your Mother" (under a photograph of Earth).

It was April 22, 1970, the first Earth Day. Twenty million people came together in cities and towns across the nation to protest the pollution that was choking the life out of the planet. People were there not just to protest but also to teach and to learn. Some of the key events of the day were teach-ins. Experts taught the public about the science behind what was happening to their world. Americans took these lessons to heart.

That evening, in a CBS News Special Report, journalist Walter Cronkite described the event as "a day dedicated to enlisting all the citizens of a bountiful country in a common cause of saving life from the deadly by-products of that bounty: the fouled skies, the filthy waters, the littered earth."[1]

The nation's skies were so fouled and its waters so filthy that in many places, it was no longer even safe to breathe the air or

Every April 22, it's Earth Day, a chance for everyone to celebrate our planet and determine its environmental course in the future.

drink the water. Biologist Barry Commoner, speaking on that day, put it like this: "This planet is threatened with destruction and we who live in it with death. The heavens reek, the waters below are foul, children die in infancy … We are in a crisis of survival."[2]

The demands for change did not stop at the end of that April day. The result of this national outpouring of concern was as effective as it was peaceful. Over the next decade, the United States Congress passed many environmental laws. The air and water became cleaner, which made the public safer. Laws were passed to protect wildlife and deal with toxic waste. Over the next few decades, these laws were sometimes strengthened and other times weakened. Those who wanted to protect the environment and the living things that depend on it struggled against those who wanted to protect the interests of business and industry.

That struggle continues today. Humanity is facing a worldwide environmental threat—perhaps the most serious crisis it has ever faced: climate change. The debate over legislation to address the problem is the central environmental issue of the twenty-first century.

Earth Day 1970 was the time when Americans first poured into the streets to demand that their leaders pass laws to protect the environment. However, the story of environmental law in the United States goes back much farther than 1970.

Burning Rivers and Raging Citizens

Americans have always loved their country's natural beauty. It contains forests, mountains, prairies, and wetlands. These areas are home to wolves, bears, alligators, eagles, mountain lions, and many more animals. However, for much of the nation's history, Americans have taken this treasure for granted.

A National Duty

When Theodore Roosevelt was a boy, he dreamed of becoming a naturalist. He especially loved to study birds, but he was fascinated by all kinds of nature and wildlife. He studied the works of great naturalists; he eagerly read the works of Charles Darwin, who published *On the Origin of Species* the year after Roosevelt was born. When Roosevelt first saw real bears—not the storybook kind that are often shown as friendly or silly— he described them as "wicked smart."[1] When he was ten years old, his family went on a yearlong tour of Europe. It was on this trip that he realized how huge and wild his home continent was. In a biography of Roosevelt, historian Douglas Brinkley

Theodore Roosevelt loved nature. When he became president, he made sure to preserve the land for future generations.

described this trip as "the beginnings of Roosevelt's imagining America as a wilderness."[2]

Roosevelt did grow up to be a naturalist—and a president of the United States. As president, he was able to do more than simply enjoy and study nature. In May of 1908, during his second term in office, Roosevelt invited state governors and experts on natural resources to a conference at the White House. The purpose of the meeting was to discuss how to protect the nation's increasingly endangered natural resources.

At the opening of the meeting, Roosevelt gave a speech called "Conservation as a National Duty." He saw protecting nature as a responsibility. In this speech, he said, "The time has come to inquire seriously what will happen when our forests are gone, when the coal, the iron, the oil, and the gas are exhausted, when the soils have still further impoverished and washed into the streams, polluting the rivers, denuding the fields and obstructing navigation."[3]

By the time Roosevelt left office in 1909, he had designated 230 million acres (93 million hectares) of wilderness as public lands. Most of it was national forests. In 1905, he created the United States Forest Service to oversee this land. He also established fifty-one wildlife refuges and made it clear to the nation that it would be a dire mistake to take nature for granted.

Roosevelt's conservation measures were the first of their kind, and they were very important. However, they only protected wilderness areas. Americans needed to do much more than that, but it took them half a century to realize just how much more.

A Disturbing Fable

Rachel Carson was born in 1907, one year before Roosevelt proclaimed that conservation was a national duty. By the time Carson was an adult, national forests and wildlife refuges were protected. However, the rest of the nation's land was in trouble. During the first few decades of the twentieth century, the United States had experienced enormous growth. Industrialization and urbanization spread across the land.

Growing up in Springdale, Pennsylvania, Carson could look out her window and see smoke spewing from the chimneys of the American Glue Factory just a mile away. The air and water of her hometown were polluted by a coal-fired power plant. Still, Carson developed a deep love of nature. When she grew up, she became a zoologist. She was a gifted writer and published many magazine articles and several best-selling books about the wonders of nature. She understood that citizens wouldn't want to protect nature if they didn't understand and love it. Carson also worked as a science editor for the US Fish and Wildlife Service (USFWS), a conservation agency established in 1940 as part of Franklin Roosevelt's New Deal. In this job, she had access to the latest scientific research—and what she saw was alarming.

In 1962, Carson published *Silent Spring*, a book that literally changed the world. She had been studying previous research

Rachel Carson, inspired by the pollution she saw in her hometown, set out to do something about it. Her book *Silent Spring* forever changed the way people viewed the world.

on how pesticides affected the environment. She was particularly interested in a pesticide known as DDT. This chemical is effective and relatively safe when used in small amounts for localized mosquito control. However, that wasn't how it was being used in the 1960s. American farmers were spraying pounds of it per acre from airplanes to control mosquitoes, fire ants, and other insects. DDT was having devastating effects throughout the food chain. The chemical not only killed insects, it also killed the birds that ate them. It was dangerous to humans as well. In *Silent Spring*, Carson explained how nature is interconnected. Killing one kind of animal—in this case, insects—has an effect on almost every other part of the environment.

In *Silent Spring*, Carson took a scientific issue and presented it in a way that would make readers emotional. The "silent spring" of the title refers to a future in which no birds sing and no insects buzz.

The book opens with a description of a town where "life seemed to live in harmony with its surroundings" until a "strange blight crept over the area." The birds and insects died. Animals and people became ill. The roadsides, Carson wrote, "were lined with brown and withered vegetation ... Silent, deserted by all living things."[4] The story of the town in the book was a fable. However, she explained that many towns had experienced at least some of the disasters she described. In the rest of the book, she explained what this strange blight, or damage, was and why it would turn all of

Chemicals used to eliminate insects can weaken the structure of eggshells, putting baby birds in danger. Can you imagine a world without birds?

A Bird-Eat-Bird World

When a bird has a large amount of DDT in its body, its eggs have very thin shells that often break before hatching. This is an especially bad problem for birds of prey, because they eat other birds. This raises the amount of DDT in their bodies. For many years, many species of birds of prey were endangered because of DDT. The bald eagle, which is the symbol of the United States, was one of these birds. DDT was banned in the United States in 1972. Many birds, including the bald eagle, are no longer considered endangered.

America into the fictional town she described if something was not done to stop it.

In the book, Carson blamed the problem on corporate greed and stated that the government cannot be trusted to adequately address the problem without pressure from individual citizens. She asked readers to organize and demand change.

The response to the book was immediate and intense. The chemical industry hit back hard. Velsicol, the company that manufactured DDT, threatened to sue Carson's publishers. Velsicol also tried to stop the Audubon Society from publishing excerpts from the book. The company's attorneys suggested that Carson was being paid by the Soviet Union to publish lies that would hurt the United States. Some of Carson's opponents also argued that her analysis of the science couldn't be trusted because she was a woman.

However, the public's response was strong, too. People were appalled by what they read—and they were moved to demand change. Rachel Carson died of breast cancer in 1964. However, her legacy lives on even today. She is widely considered the founder of the modern environmental movement.

Oozing Rivers

Pesticides raining from the sky was not the only environmental problem Americans faced in the 1960s. An article published in *Time* magazine in 1969 described how bad things had become: "The Potomac reaches the nation's capital as a pleasant stream, and leaves it stinking from the 240 million gallons of wastes that are flushed into it daily. Among other horrors ... Omaha's meat packers fill the Missouri River with animal grease balls as big as oranges." One of the nation's filthiest rivers was the Cuyahoga in Cleveland, Ohio. It "oozes rather than flows"[5] said the *Time* article.

The Cuyahoga was so littered with oil-coated garbage that it often burst into flames. Many people think the photographs of the flaming river were what turned the environmental movement from concerned policy discussions to political activism. Carson's excellent writing and thorough research had awakened a nation, and the image of a river on fire gave them the push they needed to act. Even politicians could no longer ignore the country's environmental crisis.

In 1970, the National Environmental Policy Act (NEPA) was signed into law by President Richard Nixon. It requires federal agencies to prepare detailed reports of how a proposed project will affect the environment. These reports are called environmental impact statements. It's difficult to overstate how important this legislation was. For the first time, federal agencies were required to consider the effects on the environment when planning projects, such as building roads or dams.

The Cuyahoga River in Cleveland, Ohio, was once so polluted that it often caught on fire. Thanks to cleanup efforts and environmental legislation, this is how it looks today.

Meanwhile, citizens formed a grassroots environmental movement, just as Rachel Carson wanted them to do. The first Earth Day was held in the United States only, but concern for the environment is not limited to America, and it is now a worldwide annual event.

In terms of creating change, the first Earth Day was a huge success, prompting Congress to start passing laws that were designed to protect the nation's environment. The NEPA was just the beginning.

Spacious Skies and Shining Seas

People expect scary things to happen around Halloween. However, they expect them to be imaginary. During the Halloween season of 1948, the citizens of Donora, Pennsylvania, experienced a horror that was all too real.

The Killer Fog

A few days before Halloween, Donora was engulfed in heavy fog. The town is nestled in the Monongahela River Valley, and fog is common there, but this was different. An unusual weather event called an anticyclone had trapped air near the ground. A normal fog would dissipate as the cold air near the ground circulated up and away. The anticyclone kept this fog in place. It was so dense that people in the stands at the local high school football game couldn't see the players on the field. Streetlights stayed on all day, but people still couldn't see well enough to walk down the street. Soon it became obvious that this was no ordinary fog. Houseplants shriveled and died. People began to have trouble breathing. Then people began to get sick. Before the nightmare was over, twenty-six people had died and a third of the town had become ill. What was this mysterious killer fog?

Air pollution impacts almost every large city in the world. Car emissions, factories, dust, pollen, and more contribute to clogging the air.

Donora was home to American Steel & Wire and the Donora Zinc Works. The smokestacks of the two plants released dangerous chemicals into the air each day. Sulfuric acid, nitrogen dioxide, and fluorine were just a few of the poisonous chemicals in the town's atmosphere. As long as the winds blew the nasty air away, no one really noticed it, and the factories provided good jobs for the townspeople. However, when the strange weather trapped that air and turned it into smog, which is a severe kind of air pollution, the people learned just how deadly their air was. On Halloween, rain finally washed away the smog, but the people who lived in Donora remembered it and started a movement that swept across the nation.

Take a Deep Breath

Today, Donora's slogan is "Clean Air Started Here." Immediately after the Donora smog incident, many cities and states began to pass laws to control air pollution. It took a little longer for changes to happen on the national level.

However, the federal government eventually took action. In 1955, the US Congress passed the Air Pollution Control Act. This law didn't do much to clean up the air. It simply stated that research into air pollution should take place, and it provided funds for studies. Eight years later, the federal government passed legislation that was aimed at making a real difference. The Clean Air Act of 1963 limited the amount and kind of emissions that could be released by factories, such as power plants and steel mills.

Over the next few years, several amendments changed the law to make it more comprehensive, adding standards for automobile emissions and setting air quality standards and deadlines for meeting these regulations.

In 1970, President Richard Nixon created the Environmental Protection Agency (EPA) to help manage and enforce these

In cities such as Beijing, China, many residents wear masks to make breathing easier. Air pollution impacts many health conditions, such as asthma.

new environmental laws. It is the EPA's job to develop and enforce environmental regulations. The EPA also helps state governments in their efforts to design their own environmental policies and to meet the federal standards.

Get the Lead Out

In 1970, the Clean Air Act was amended again in a much more dramatic way. The 1970 law set higher standards for air quality and increased limits on emissions. It also made it easier for the government to enforce these new regulations. Furthermore, the 1970 amendment addressed another serious problem in the nation's air: a chemical called lead.

Lead was in the air mainly because it was added to gasoline. It made car engines run better, but the effect on people was not good: Exposure to lead has terrible effects on the human central nervous system. Lead is especially dangerous for children because eating or breathing it can cause many developmental problems. When gasoline contained lead, exhaust fumes from cars spewed the dangerous chemical into the air, creating a massive public health hazard. The 1970 Clean Air Act gradually phased out the use of lead in gasoline. By 1995, leaded gasoline was completely banned.

The Clean Air Act was not amended during the 1980s. The government was more focused on economic growth than on protecting the environment. However, in 1990, the law was again amended to strengthen and improve environmental regulations. The 1990 amendment specifically addressed two pressing issues: acid rain and the ozone layer.

About 9 miles (15 kilometers) above Earth's surface, there is a concentration of a gas called ozone in the atmosphere. This is called the ozone layer. The ozone layer absorbs some of

Lead Is Back

In 2014, the city of Flint, Michigan, switched its water supply from Lake Michigan to the Flint River. The river water damaged lead pipes, causing lead to leak into the water. Children who lived in Flint were found to have dangerous levels of the chemical in their blood. In 2016, President Barack Obama declared a national emergency and authorized $5 million to help the city. In 2017, the city's water was officially declared safe to drink, but as of 2019, an estimated 2,500 lead service lines still existed in the city.

The ozone layer absorbs most of the sun's harmful radiation. Chemicals in our air break the ozone layer apart and let more of these damaging rays reach Earth's surface.

the sun's radiation, which can cause sunburn and skin cancer. By the 1960s, the ozone layer had become very thin in places, allowing dangerous amounts of ultraviolet radiation to reach Earth. In 1974, scientists discovered that a group of chemicals, called chlorofluorocarbons (CFCs), were destroying the ozone layer. CFCs were most commonly used in refrigerators, air conditioners, and aerosol sprays. In 1987, most of the world's nations, including the United States and Canada, signed the Montreal Protocol. This was an agreement to greatly reduce worldwide emissions of CFCs. Everyone knew it would take a long time for the ozone layer to make a comeback. Still, the only way for that to happen was to eliminate the chemicals that were destroying it. The plan is working: According to the EPA, the ozone layer should be completely restored by the middle of the twenty-first century.[1]

When the air is very polluted with chemicals such as sulphur and nitrogen, rain becomes too acidic. Acid rain can cause trees and plants to die. It also adds more pollution to rivers and lakes. The 1990 amendment to the Clean Air Act mandated a reduction in emissions of chemicals that cause acid rain. This law, like the Montreal Protocol, was extremely effective. It reduced emissions of the chemicals responsible for acid rain by 50 percent.[2]

Don't Drink the Water

Acid rain wasn't the biggest source of trouble for the nation's waterways. For decades, rivers had been treated as a handy way to dispose of industrial waste. In an article published in the *Allegheny Front*, Julie Grant talked with people who lived near Cleveland's Cuyahoga River. "All of the industries ... just dumped their waste in the river— untreated," Ben Stefanski, who had once been utilities director of

Cleveland, told Grant. "That was just what the river was there for. We didn't think about the future."[3]

By the 1970s, a lot of people had begun thinking about the future, and they were getting worried. Press coverage of

Before the Clean Water Act, rivers and lakes were clogged with pollution and trash. Now that most of them are clearner, the focus has turned to Earth's oceans.

the Cuyahoga River fire helped spread that concern. Americans began putting enormous pressure on their leaders to clean up the environment—and the government responded. In 1972, the US Congress passed a major overhaul of a 1948 law called the Federal Water Pollution Control Act. After these amendments, the law became known as the Clean Water Act (CWA).

The text of the CWA begins with these words: "The objective of this Act is to restore and maintain the chemical, physical, and biological integrity of the Nation's waters."[4] This was an ambitious goal in a nation where rivers had a tendency to burst into flames, but the CWA was ambitious legislation. It gave the government the authority to regulate the amount of pollution factories could dump into the nation's lakes and rivers. It also gave the government the authority to set standards for water quality. Any factory, local government, or other entity that discharged pollutants into the water had to get a government permit and abide by strict regulations. The CWA also provided funds for building wastewater treatment plants and other clean water initiatives.

The water that came out of people's faucets needed some work, too. In 1974, Congress passed the Safe Drinking Water Act. This law gives the government the responsibility of setting standards for drinking water quality. All state and local governments that provide drinking water to the public must meet these standards. Amendments continued to update both acts in keeping with new scientific discoveries and changes in industry and technology.

In his 1970 State of the Union address, President Richard Nixon said, "The great question of the seventies is ... shall we make our peace with nature and begin to make reparations for the damage we have done to our air, to our land, and to our water?"[5] The Clean Air Act, the Clean Water Act, and other legislation passed in that decade were significant attempts to make those reparations.

What Shall We Do with All This Poison?

Thanks to Rachel Carson's efforts, the United States government banned DDT in 1972. However, DDT was only a tiny fraction of the dangerous chemicals in the environment. While DDT was raining from the sky, a dangerous black sludge was oozing from underground.

A Dream Goes Bad

In 1892, William T. Love wanted to build a model city. He envisioned a perfect community with happy and prosperous citizens. His plan was to build a short canal between the upper and lower parts of the Niagara River. This would create

Old barrels of waste still litter our planet. Chemicals, once they have been made and used, cannot be discarded without thought, and burying waste often leads to bigger problems later.

a beautiful waterfall that would be a source of inexpensive electricity for the community of half a million people. He promised free electricity to companies that located there. Someone wrote a song about the project, sung to the tune of "Yankee Doodle": "They're building now a great big ditch through dirt and rock so gritty / They say 'twill make all very rich who live in Model City."[1]

Love began excavating the canal but didn't get far. An economic depression ruined the project's financing. Better technology for transmitting electricity took away its primary selling point. By 1910, all there was to show of Model City was a large ditch. Love's canal was about 1 mile (1.6 km) long, about 20 yards (18 meters) wide, and ranged from 10 to 40 feet (3 to 12 m) deep.

In 1920, Hooker Chemical Company bought the land. The half-built canal was a handy place to dump waste. Over the next three decades, the company filled the canal with 55-gallon (208-liter) metal containers, or drums. The drums were filled with a variety of dangerous chemicals. A 1979 article in *The Atlantic* described the contents of Love Canal as a "witch's brew of compounds of truly remarkable toxicity."[2] When the ditch was full, they simply covered it with topsoil.

In 1953, Hooker donated the land to the Niagara Falls Board of Education so the city could build an elementary school there. The playground of the school was built directly over the canal. Many new homes were built near the school, and young families moved in. It wasn't a model city, but it was a very nice working-class neighborhood. It was called Love Canal after the abandoned project. However, the reality ended up being very far from William Love's dream.

The waste in the canal began to seep out in the 1970s. Families found black slime in their basements. Backyards became bubbling pits of stinking goop. As the ground level sank, the tops of drums containing the toxic brew began to emerge. Children came in from recess with stinging eyes and chemical burns on their skin. At first, people didn't understand just how dangerous these chemicals could be. Soon, however, they realized this was more than just a nasty smell. Babies were born with birth defects. Rashes, headaches, and neurological complaints were common. Many citizens suffered from liver damage. Many of the chemicals oozing from the canal were known to cause cancer.

At first, the government—both local and federal—was slow to act. However, in the spring of 1978, the New York State health commissioner declared the area hazardous, and families were evacuated. The governor of New York announced that the state would buy the homes. President Jimmy Carter approved emergency financial aid to help people relocate.

Cleaning Up the Mess

Eckardt Beck was an EPA administrator between 1977 and 1979. He wrote, "Quite simply, Love Canal is one of the most appalling environmental tragedies in American history. What is worse is that it cannot be regarded as an isolated event. It could happen again—anywhere in this country—unless we move expeditiously to prevent it."[3] Beck was right. There were hundreds more sites like Love Canal around the country.

In 1980, Congress reacted to the problem by passing the Comprehensive Environmental Response, Compensation, and Liability Act (CERCLA). The law is more commonly known as Superfund. This is because the law created a fund for cleaning up hazardous waste sites. The Superfund works like this: A citizen notifies the EPA when a toxic waste site is suspected. The EPA investigates and gives the site a score based on how dangerous the site is.

Environmental pollution is everywhere. In 1989, the *Exxon Valdez* tanker spilled oil into Alaska's Prince William Sound. About 1,300 miles (2,100 km) of coastline were impacted. The spill led to the Oil Pollution Act of 1990.

This determination is based on how nasty the chemicals are and how close the site is to where people live and work.

If the score is fairly low, the site is designated a remedial site. Remedial sites are scheduled for long-term cleanup. Landfills and abandoned plants are often remedial sites. If the score is high, the site is declared a removal site. Removals are typically emergency situations, such as spills from oil tankers or factory fires. In 1986, the Superfund Amendments and Reauthorization Act (SARA) made some changes to the original law. Among other things, it increased states' involvement in the cleanup process. It also encouraged more citizen participation in decision-making.

CERCLA requires companies that are responsible for the pollution to pay for the cleanup. However, it is not always possible to identify the responsible companies, and sometimes companies can get out of having to pay by proving that they

Toxic Flooding

Human negligence is not the only way toxic chemicals spread. In 2017, Hurricane Harvey caused severe flooding in Houston, Texas. Thirteen Superfund sites were flooded during the hurricane. This put the surrounding communities at risk of being poisoned by the contaminated water. Superfund sites were also in the path of Hurricanes Katrina, Sandy, and Irma. As storms become worse and more frequent due to climate change and rising sea levels increase the risk of flooding, the EPA is working to determine how to protect communities from storms that spread toxic waste.

tried to prevent the disaster. For these reasons, a tax on crude oil and chemicals was originally used to collect money for the Superfund. The law authorizing these taxes expired in 1995. After that, money for cleanups has often come out of the government's general budget.

Many Superfund sites have been so successfully cleaned up that they can be safely returned to the public. Houses, office buildings, and new factories have been built on former Superfund sites. Other Superfund sites have been turned into wetlands. Love Canal was declared safe in 2004. Some of the houses in the community were renovated and sold to new owners. The neighborhood was renamed Black Creek Village. However, more chemicals have been found, and the people who remained or have moved back to the area are concerned that the chemicals under the ground near Love Canal may be coming back.

Strong Laws and Weak Ones

Clearly it wasn't a good idea to build a community on top of a ditch full of dangerous chemicals, but what *should* we do with the poisons that are so often by-products of industry? Congress addressed that issue in 1976 with the Resources Conservation and Recovery Act (RCRA).

This law provides very specific requirements for dealing with solid and hazardous wastes, starting from when they are created to when they are disposed of. CERCLA was designed to clean up already contaminated storage sites; RCRA aims to provide guidelines and practices that stop the problem before it starts.

In 1986, RCRA was updated and strengthened by the Hazardous and Solid Waste Amendments (HSWA). HSWA gradually phased out the practice of disposing of solid wastes in landfills. Like much environmental legislation, RCRA has been

People continue to speak up and protest about protecting the planet and its environment. If we pollute this planet, we can't pack up and head to another one.

amended several times over the years. This is necessary to keep up with changing technology.

Laws were also enacted to try to limit the dangerous chemicals themselves. In 1976, Congress passed the Toxic Substances Control Act (TSCA). This law was intended to investigate new chemicals to make sure they are safe before allowing them to be used. However, it has been the subject of a great deal of criticism over the years. When the law was written, it allowed chemicals that were already on the market to remain there. This amounted to 62,000 chemicals. Only 200 of those have since been studied, and only 5 banned.[4] In addition, the EPA couldn't require a company to test a new chemical unless the EPA could show the substance might pose a risk. Of course, the EPA can't know that without the tests. These sorts of limits made TSCA a very weak law. The 2008–2009 annual report of the President's Cancer Panel says that TSCA "may be the most egregious example of ineffective regulation of environmental contaminants."[5] To address these issues, amendments to TSCA were passed in 2016 with overwhelming support in Congress. The new law is called the Frank R. Lautenberg Chemical Safety for the 21st Century Act.

Thanks to the Superfund and RCRA, many poisons have been removed from the environment or safely stored. However, the EPA is still working to protect the nation from dangerous chemicals in the future.

Where Man Is a Visitor

Environmental laws have done a great deal to protect people. However, humans aren't the only creatures that need protection. When Americans realized that the environment was in trouble, they didn't just think of themselves. They took steps to protect animals, plants, and entire ecosystems as well.

This Land Is Your Land

Aldo Leopold loved nature from the time he was a small child. When he grew up, he studied forestry and wildlife management. After graduation, he went to work with the United States Forest Service and quickly became the nation's top expert in wildlife management. He also changed the way people thought about the wilderness.

When Leopold joined the Forest Service in 1909, most people believed that humans should control nature. Theodore Roosevelt loved nature and wanted to protect it, but his aim was to conserve nature for the benefit of humans. He wanted people to be able to hunt and hike

Part of the Forestry Service's job is to maintain lands after wildfires. Shown here are forest flowers blooming two years after a wildfire in Colorado.

and watch birds. Another goal of conservation was to protect resources humans used, such as oil and timber.

During his years working with nature and wildlife, Leopold came to see the role of humans in nature much differently. He wrote, "We abuse land because we regard it as a commodity belonging to us. When we see land as a community to which we belong, we may begin to use it with love and respect."[1] Leopold defined "land" as a community that included soil, water, plants, and animals—including humans. Taking care of the land required understanding the complex relationships among all the parts of the community.

In 1935, Leopold helped found the Wilderness Society, a nonprofit conservation organization that works to protect natural areas and public lands. Since it was created, the organization has worked to create a balanced use of public lands. This means that extraction of resources, such as oil and timber, is balanced with the protection of the land's ecosystems and its availability for recreation by the public—the people who own the land.

As It Was in the Beginning

In the early 1930s, Howard Zahniser took a job with the Wilderness Society. His first role there was as executive secretary and editor of the organization's magazine, *Living Wilderness.*

Soon after coming to the society, Zahniser was involved in a campaign by environmentalists to prevent a dam from being built on the Green River in Dinosaur National Monument in Colorado. The environmentalists won that battle. However, Zahniser realized that if nothing was done, preserving wilderness would become an ongoing series of "overlapping emergencies, threats and defense campaigns."[2]

He worked to develop legislation that would protect large areas of land before the emergencies occurred. In May 1956, he completed the first draft of a bill to establish a national wilderness preservation system. The bill outlined appropriate use for protected areas and listed potential new areas for protection.

Zahniser worked tirelessly to get the bill passed. It took eight years and sixty-six revisions. However, in September 1964, the Wilderness Act was finally signed into law. In the act, Zahniser wrote that a wilderness, "in contrast with those areas where

The Green River in Dinosaur National Monument continues to flow as it always has, preserving the natural beauty of the area.

man and his own works dominate the landscape, is hereby recognized as an area where the earth and its community of life are untrammeled by man, where man himself is a visitor who does not remain."[3]

The law designated certain areas that were already publicly owned lands as wilderness areas. This designation gives these areas even more protection than parks and national forests. Motorized vehicles and even bicycles are prohibited in wilderness areas. As the law states, humans can visit, but they must not do anything that interferes with the natural development of those areas.

When President Lyndon Johnson signed the Wilderness Act into law, he said, "If future generations are to remember us with gratitude rather than contempt, we must leave them a glimpse of the world as it was in the beginning, not just after we got through with it."[4]

As of 2019, the United States government owns and manages about 640 million acres (260 million ha) of land. That means nearly a third of the US landmass is public land.[5] Several government agencies—the National Park Service (NPS), the Forest Service, the Fish and Wildlife Service, and the Bureau of Land Management (BLM)—take care of this land for the American people. How the land is designated determines how it can be used. For example, land designated as a national park is only minorly changed to make it easier for people to visit. However, land managed by the BLM is often used for logging and mining.

Mammoths (shown here) roamed the world millions of years ago and have since gone extinct, but many species remain endangered today because of changing environments.

Wilderness areas, which are managed by the Forest Service and covered by the Wilderness Act, are the most protected of all.

Making a List

Species go extinct all the time. It's a natural process. However, this generally happens slowly over time. When many species go

45

extinct in a relatively short period of time, it is called a mass extinction. As far as researchers can tell, this has happened only five times in the history of life on Earth. Because many species have not yet been well studied, it can be difficult to make accurate estimates of extinction rates. However, many scientists think Earth is in the middle of a sixth mass extinction.[6] Thanks to human activity, the current rate of extinction is hundreds or even thousands of times higher than the natural rate would be.[7] In a study published in 2015 in the journal *Science Advanced*, researchers wrote:

> The evidence is incontrovertible that recent extinction rates are unprecedented in human history and highly unusual in Earth's history. Our analysis emphasizes that our global society has started to destroy species of other organisms at an accelerating rate, initiating a mass extinction episode unparalleled for 65 million years.[8]

Just How Bad Is It?

For a species to be listed under the Endangered Species Act as "endangered," it must be in danger of extinction throughout most of its range. To be listed as "threatened," a species must be likely to become endangered in the near future in all or most of its range. Scientists use both scientific and commercial data (such as fishing catches) to determine which species make the lists. However, when making decisions about what species are in danger, they cannot consider the economic impact of adding a species to the list.

Decades before scientists began warning of a sixth extinction, they knew that the loss of biodiversity was an increasingly dangerous problem. In the 1960s and 1970s, as the environmental movement gained momentum, Americans became aware of this looming crisis. In 1969, Congress passed the Endangered Species Conservation Act. It was an amendment to an earlier law, the Endangered Species Conservation Act of 1966. The amendment added some animal species to a list of animals protected by the 1966 act and prohibited importing foreign endangered animals.

In 1973, Congress replaced those laws with the Endangered Species Act (ESA). It defined "endangered" and "threatened," expanded earlier protections of specific animals, and included all endangered species or those likely to soon become endangered. The list was no longer limited to animals but included endangered plants and invertebrates as well.

Trade-Offs

The Endangered Species Act has brought many species back from the brink of extinction. Just a few of these are the California condor, the gray wolf, the humpback whale, the American alligator, the grizzly bear, and the bald eagle.

However, the legislation has been criticized as well. Some environmentalists think that the ESA focuses too much on large, high-profile species, such as grizzly bears and whales. It does not, they say, do enough to protect the ecosystems those species are part of.

Another very serious criticism of the ESA is that protecting animals can sometimes cause problems for humans. The story of the northern spotted owl is a good example. This type of owl lives in the old-growth forests of the Pacific Northwest. Over the last 150 years, logging companies have cut timber from these forests, leaving fewer and fewer places for the owls to live.

When the northern spotted owl was designated as "threatened" in 1990, the way we managed their habitat changed.

Now, only about 10 percent of these forests are left.[9]

In 1986, environmentalists asked the US government to list the northern spotted owl as endangered. This would have kept the timber companies from clearing what remained of the forests. The timber companies sued to keep the owl off the list. They pointed out that if they could not cut timber from these forests, thousands of people who work as loggers or in lumber mills would lose their jobs.

In 1990, the owl was classified as "threatened," restricting which areas could be logged but not completely eliminating all timber cutting in the area. Protection of other flora and fauna, such as a small fish called the snail darter; a tiny wildflower known as the furbish lousewort; and whales, dolphins, and tortoises have caused similar conflicts. Protecting nonhuman species and the ecosystems they live in often requires a careful balancing with the needs of humans.

It's Getting Hot in Here

America's rivers are no longer bursting into flames. Birds still sing in the spring. Many animals around the world have been removed from the endangered species list. However, the entire planet now faces what is probably the greatest environmental crisis in the history of humanity: global warming. Politicians and citizens alike are debating what laws might be needed to address this serious problem.

A Long, Slow Burn

Guy Stewart Callendar was a steam engineer and an amateur climatologist. He spent several years collecting the previous

The world is witnessing climate change like never before. When Arctic ice breaks up, it changes how polar bears hunt and roam.

century's temperature data from weather stations around the world. Then—working with pencil and paper—he averaged all these readings to get the average global temperature over that period. He published the results in 1938. This clearly showed that Earth's average temperature had been steadily increasing. The increase was far more than could be accounted for by normal processes. Things had begun to heat up more quickly during the Industrial Revolution, when more carbon dioxide started being released into the atmosphere. These emissions come primarily from burning fossil fuels used to generate electricity, heat and cool buildings, and power automobiles, factories, and so on. It took many more years and a lot of study, but the evidence grew stronger. Earth is getting dangerously warmer, and the increase in carbon emissions is a major factor.

The Intergovernmental Panel on Climate Change (IPCC) is a group of thousands of scientists from around the world. They have been analyzing climate change since 1988. Every few years, they issue a report that assesses the current science and the potential impact of climate change. According to the IPCC, future effects of climate change will include hotter average global temperatures (though some places may see cooler temperatures at times), more flooding in some areas, and more droughts in others. They also say that hurricanes and tornados will become stronger. Sea levels are expected to rise between 1 and 4 feet (0.3 and 1.2 m) by the year 2100.[1]

In January of 2019, the US Department of Defense issued a report, saying, "The effects of a changing climate are a national security issue."[2] Among other things, the report notes that many military installations surveyed are already experiencing effects related to climate change. The report specifically mentions flooding, drought, and wildfires.

The United States government has taken steps to protect the environment, but different administrations have different goals—leading to uneven policies and continued protests from a concerned public.

The Bill That Wouldn't Pass

Despite this looming catastrophe, there have been no laws designed to deal with it.

In 1990, the US Congress passed an amendment to the Clean Air Act that created a cap-and-trade program meant to address the problem of acid rain. This program put a limit (a cap) on how much pollution a given business can produce. At the same time, it allowed businesses to buy and sell (trade) permits to produce pollution.

For example, if a polluter doesn't put out enough pollution to meet its cap, it can sell the rest of its credit to another company. If it uses up its allowed amount of pollution, it can buy more from a company that has some to spare. The cap-and-trade program for acid rain was a surprising success. By 2003, the country was on track to halve emissions of the pollution that caused acid rain.[3]

In 2003, US senators John McCain and Joe Lieberman introduced a bill to apply the cap-and-trade model to carbon emissions. McCain said, "Too much attention has been focused on the uncertainties and not enough on what is known in tackling the problem at hand. It's time for the U.S. to do its part."[4] However, the US did not do its part. The bill did not pass. It was reintroduced two more times, in 2005 and in 2007. Each time, it got less support than the previous time. In 2009, a carbon cap-and-trade bill finally did pass narrowly in the House of Representatives. However, it did not pass in the Senate.

Let's Get Together

Like protecting animals, addressing climate change can't be done by one nation alone. Global warming affects the entire world, so the entire world will have to work together to solve the problem. In 1997, representatives from forty-one nations gathered in Kyoto, Japan, to address the problem of global warming. The agreement they made was called the Kyoto Protocol. The nations that signed the agreement committed to reducing their greenhouse gas emissions. These reductions would start in 2008 and continue until 2012. According to the protocol, countries that produced a lot of emissions would aim for a greater percentage reduction in emissions than countries with less industry. Nations that were just beginning to develop an industrial economy were not expected to reduce their emissions at all.

Greenhouse effect

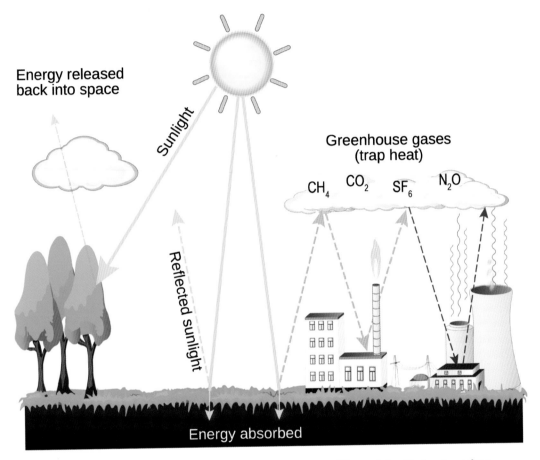

Energy released back into space

Sunlight

Greenhouse gases (trap heat)

CH_4 CO_2 SF_6 N_2O

Reflected sunlight

Energy absorbed

Greenhouse gases emitted from cars and factories trap more of the sun's heat in the atmosphere instead of releasing it back into space. This causes the planet to warm.

There were a few problems with the plan. One was that China was not expected to reduce its emissions at all. That was because China was considered a developing nation. However, because of its large population, it was the world's biggest emitter of greenhouse gases. The United States was the second-largest emitter of greenhouse gases, but it refused to sign the deal, so the Kyoto Protocol went into effect without the two largest offenders on board. As a result, many other nations either dropped out or failed to meet their obligations under the agreement.

In 2015, the world's nations met again, this time in Paris, France. Things went much better this time around.

We'll Always Have Paris (or Maybe We Won't)

On December 12, 2015, in Paris, France, a roomful of normally serious and dignified diplomats from around the world leapt to their feet, cheering and hugging one another. Two famous Paris monuments—the Eiffel Tower and the Arc de Triomphe—were lit up with green spotlights. The cause of such celebration was a historic climate agreement. Representatives from United Nations member states had just finalized an agreement to take serious action to slow global warming. The best part was that both China and the United States were taking part.

The Paris Agreement says, "Climate change represents an urgent and potentially irreversible threat to human societies and the planet and thus requires the widest possible cooperation by all countries."[5] Realizing this, it sets ambitious goals. Nations that signed the deal agreed to keep average global temperatures from rising more than 2 degrees Celsius

(3.6 degrees Fahrenheit) above what those temperatures had been before the Industrial Revolution.

Two degrees doesn't sound like much, but that much of an increase above the average temperature before the Industrial Revolution would be significant. It's the point where climate experts expect disastrous changes to Earth's climate. These

If left unaddressed, climate change could lead to rising waters from melting glaciers and a change in coastlines.

We'll Do This Ourselves

In 2017, the United States abandoned the Paris Agreement. Other nations are struggling to meet their commitments to the plan. However, while nations dither, many cities are doing their part. Cities Climate Leadership Group (C40) is a network of more than ninety cities around the world. Cities such as Paris, New York, Mexico City, Boston, Tokyo, and Copenhagen are taking upon themselves the job of reducing emissions of greenhouse gases. What large governments can't do, sometimes small ones can.

include higher sea levels submerging coastal cities and island nations, devastating droughts and wildfires, more frequent and more severe storms, and a dramatic increase in the extinction rate. These things are already beginning to happen. The 2°C mark could be the point of no return.

The Paris Agreement also takes into account social justice. The text of the agreement acknowledges that the people most threatened by climate change are those least responsible for causing it. Rich countries got rich in large part by reckless use of fossil fuels. In Paris, these nations agreed to give billions of dollars of aid to poor countries. This aid is intended to help poor countries expand their economies without relying on carbon-heavy industries the way richer nations did.

The Paris Agreement isn't perfect. Each nation is left to decide how to meet its targets. There are no punishments for failing to do so. Some experts think that even if the world does manage to stay below a 2°C increase, it won't be enough. Still, the Paris Agreement is a start—and far more than has ever been done before.

When the Paris Agreement was worked out, the United States government set targets for reducing emissions by replacing fossil fuels with renewable energy. It also planned to take steps to make renewable energy more affordable.

However, since then, the world's second-greatest carbon emitter has indicated that it wants to drop out of the agreement. In 2017, newly elected US president Donald Trump announced that the United States would no longer participate. One of the worst things about the United States pulling out of the Paris Agreement is that it weakens an international cooperation that took decades of diplomatic work to achieve.

However, there is still hope. For one thing, the United States can't legally get out of the agreement until 2020, so US delegations are continuing to attend international meetings about this issue. Furthermore, other countries are still working to meet their Paris targets, and many US states and cities are also committed to reducing emissions—even if the federal government isn't on board.

Two Steps Forward, One Step Back

After the surge of environmental legislation in the 1970s, things slowed down quite a bit. Amendments to existing laws were made from time to time, but many of the laws designed to protect the environment were weakened and enforcement was often neglected. Despite these recurring setbacks, the nation has made a lot of progress.

What Happened to the Solar Panels?

During the 1960s and 1970s, under Presidents Richard Nixon, Gerald Ford, and Jimmy Carter, the US government appeared willing to do what was necessary to protect the environment. By the end of the 1970s, it seemed as if the United States was committed to caring for the natural world.

Things changed in 1981 when Ronald Reagan became president. In his campaign, Reagan promised "an end to restrictive controls, so we can use all the resources now available to us—including more of the oil and natural gas we have in the U.S."[1]

The previous president, Jimmy Carter, had spoken of the need to make sacrifices to address the nation's problems. He encouraged cutting back on the use of fossil fuels. Carter even installed solar panels on the White House roof. Reagan assured the public that everything would be just fine. He said Carter's talk of sacrifice and conservation was unnecessary and too gloomy. He had the solar panels removed to fix a roof leak but never had them reinstalled. Then he set about shifting the emphasis from protecting the environment to protecting the interests of business and industry.

One of Reagan's first acts in office was to severely cut the budget of the EPA. He also cut funds for renewable energy. His first EPA administrator was Anne Gorsuch, who filled

What can you do to protect our environment? What steps can you take in your daily life to make the world a better place to live in?

key positions at the EPA with people from the very industries the agency was meant to regulate. Under her leadership, employment at the EPA was cut by 22 percent. The agency's research and development budget was cut by 45 percent. Furthermore, by 1982, the EPA's enforcement had fallen by 73 percent from 1977 levels.[2] An article in the *Washington Post* at that time reported that the "cuts are so massive that they could mean a basic retreat on all the environmental programs of the past 10 years."[3]

Eventually, Gorsuch was involved in a scandal and forced to resign. She was replaced by William Ruckelshaus. Ruckelshaus had been the agency's first administrator under President Nixon. When he came back to the EPA, he told the people who worked there that the agency was "going to respect science and the scientific method" and "carry out the mission of the agency."[4] He began undoing some of the damage Gorsuch had done.

Wins and Losses

For the next three decades, there were wins and there were losses on environmental issues. It often seemed that the government would give one thing while taking away something else.

The Global Change Research Act of 1990 required the president to establish a research program made up of several science agencies. This group is required to present a report to Congress every four years that details the current status and consequences of climate change. This has been very important in keeping Congress and the public informed about climate science and the likely effects of global warming.

Soon enough, however, another antiregulatory mood swept the government. In 1994, a group of lawmakers proposed what they called a "Contract with America." Among other things, the contract proposed decreasing government regulation in many areas. Although it said nothing about the environment, putting

Hurricane Katrina hit the Gulf Coast in 2005 and marked a change in storm strength and damage. As the climate continues to change, storms are predicted to get stronger.

all of these plans into practice would have made it harder for the EPA to do its job.

In the 2000s, the EPA suffered severe budget cuts, and previously protected wilderness areas were opened up to oil and gas exploration. However, in 2005, Hurricane Katrina got everyone's attention. This unusually fierce hurricane caused a record amount of flooding and gave the nation a preview of what global warming might bring. For a while, it seemed that the country was ready to seriously address climate change. In 2015, the White House introduced the Clean Power Plan. This was the first American law aimed at reducing the amount of carbon emissions from coal-fired power plants—one of the country's biggest sources of carbon dioxide. However, the Trump administration reversed course on environmentalism.

From 2016 on, in addition to pulling out of the Paris Agreement, the US government took steps to weaken environmental protections, saying they stall economic growth. The Clean Power Plan and other environmental regulations were rolled back. Logging and drilling on public lands increased. The EPA's budget, which had been increased, was slashed again. The White House ended NASA's climate monitoring program and moved to weaken the Endangered Species Act.

Congress Is Still Listening

These ups and down can be frustrating for people who care about protecting the environment. However, overall the trend has been good. According to polls, the majority of Americans believe the government should do more to protect the environment, and elected officials know this.[5, 6]

In October 2018, Congress passed the Save Our Seas Act. This legislation is an important step toward cleaning up debris—especially plastic—from the ocean. The law reauthorized the National Oceanic and Atmospheric Administration's (NOAA) Marine Debris Program. It also encouraged the US State Department to work with other nations around the world to stop more trash from being dumped into the ocean.

In March of 2019, Congress passed legislation to protect millions of acres of wilderness and hundreds of miles of waterways. The package of laws also included a permanent reauthorization of the Land and Water Conservation Fund (LWCF). This program was established in 1964 but had expired

Oceans are littered with trash, especially plastic. In 2019, businesses worldwide began to ban plastic straws, but they are part of a much larger problem that industry will need to keep fighting.

in 2018. It uses money earned from offshore energy development to buy land and to establish and maintain state and local parks throughout the country.

US environmental laws are proving surprisingly sturdy, too. The nation's courts have, in many cases, stepped in to stop actions by the government that would violate environmental laws. For instance, in March 2019, a US district court ruled that the Interior Department was in violation of federal law when it allowed oil and gas drilling on public lands without considering the effect on climate change.

A New Spin on an Old Idea

During the Great Depression, President Franklin Roosevelt began a program called the New Deal. It was a bold plan to address the economic crisis. Eighty-six years later, in 2019, a group of congressional representatives proposed a similarly bold plan to address the crisis of global warming. They called it the Green New Deal. The program promised to cut greenhouse gas emissions to zero over a period of ten years. It would provide 100 percent of the nation's energy from clean, renewable, zero-emissions sources.

The Kids Go to Court

In 1970, young people took to the streets to protest what was happening to their environment. In 2015, they went to court. Twenty-one young people ages eight to nineteen filed a lawsuit against the US government over its climate change policies. The suit argued that by taking actions that have contributed to climate change, the government has "violated the youngest generation's constitutional rights to life, liberty, and property, as well as failed to protect essential public trust resources."[7] The lawsuit demands that the government take action to reduce carbon emissions. As of August 2019, the case is still in the courts. However it turns out, it sends a powerful message to the government from voters of the future.

Democratic lawmakers such as Alexandria Ocasio-Cortez (*center*) and Ed Markey (*right*) have big proposals for a cleaner environment. Just as with the creation of national parks, it will take bold thinking to ensure the planet's health.

The plan calls for upgrading the nation's buildings to make them more efficient, overhauling the transportation system to eliminate pollution, and much more. While many lawmakers support these policies, many others are fighting them, so it is unclear how many of the proposals in the Green New Deal will become law. Even as the Green New Deal is being discussed, laws are being passed that protect businesses at the expense of the environment. However, the fact that such a dramatic response to global warming is even being discussed shows that many Americans are ready to get serious about climate change.

We've Made Progress

In February 2019, John D. Dingell died. Dingell had been the longest-serving member of the US House of Representatives in American history. He was behind much of the landmark environmental legislation passed during the fifty-nine years he served his country. The day he died, he wrote a final note to the nation he served for so long:

> Not five decades ago, much of the largest group of freshwater lakes on Earth—our own Great Lakes—were closed to swimming and fishing and other recreational pursuits because of chemical and bacteriological contamination from untreated industrial and wastewater disposal. Today, the Great Lakes are so hospitable to marine life that one of our biggest challenges is controlling the invasive species that have made them their new home ...
>
> Hazardous wastes were dumped on empty plots in the dead of night. There were few if any restrictions on industrial emissions. We had only the barest scientific knowledge of the long-term consequences of any of this ... All of these challenges were addressed by Congress. Maybe not as fast as we wanted, or as perfectly as hoped. The work is certainly not finished. But we've made progress.[8]

Reading those words reminded Americans just how far the nation had come since Rachel Carson wrote *Silent Spring*, since the Cuyahoga River burst into flames, and since Donora, Pennsylvania, was enveloped in smog. Decades of legislation have addressed these problems and many more. There is still much work to do. However, those environmental laws have made the world a much safer and better place.

1905   President Theodore Roosevelt creates the Bureau of Forestry, beginning his legacy of wilderness protection.

1935   The Wilderness Society is founded.

1948   Dangerous smog engulfs the town of Donora, Pennsylvania.

1955   The United States passes the Air Pollution Control Act.

1962   Rachel Carson publishes *Silent Spring*.

1963   The Clean Air Act is passed.

1964   The Wilderness Act becomes law.

1970   The National Environmental Policy Act becomes law.

1970   President Richard Nixon creates the Environmental Protection Agency.

1972   The Clean Water Act becomes law.

1972   Most uses of DDT are banned in the United States.

1973   Congress passes the Endangered Species Act.

1974   The Safe Drinking Water Act is passed.

1976   Congress passes the Resources Conservation and Recovery Act (RCRA) and the Toxic Substances Control Act (TSCA).

1978   Love Canal is declared hazardous and families are evacuated.

1980   The Comprehensive Environmental Response and Liability Act (CERCLA), also known as Superfund, is passed.

1986   RCRA is updated and strengthened.

1987   Most of the world's nations, including the United States, sign the Montreal Protocol, an agreement to reduce emissions of chemicals that damage the ozone layer.

1990   The Clean Air Act is amended to address acid rain and the ozone layer.

1990   The Global Change Research Act is passed.

1997 The world's nations meet in Kyoto, Japan, to work out an agreement to reduce carbon emissions in order to slow global warming.

2009 A carbon cap-and-trade bill finally passes the US House of Representatives but fails to pass in the Senate.

2015 The Paris Agreement to fight global warming is announced.

2017 Rains from Hurricane Harvey flood thirteen Superfund sites.

2017 The United States pulls out of the Paris Agreement.

2018 The US Congress passes the Save Our Seas Act.

2019 Congress passes legislation to protect millions of additional wilderness acres.

CHAPTER NOTES

Introduction

1. CBS News, "Earth Day: A Question of Survival," April 22, 1970, www.youtube.com/watch?v=WbwC281uzUs.
2. CBS News, "Earth Day: A Question of Survival."

CHAPTER 1: Burning Rivers and Raging Citizens

1. Douglas Brinkley, *The Wilderness Warrior: Theodore Roosevelt and the Crusade for America* (New York: HarperCollins e-books, Kindle edition, 2009), p. 34.
2. Brinkley, *The Wilderness Warrior: Theodore Roosevelt and the Crusade for America*, p. 37.
3. Theodore Roosevelt, "Conservation as a National Duty," speech, May 13, 1908, Voice of Democracy: The US Oratory Project, voicesofdemocracy.umd.edu/theodore-roosevelt-conservation-as-a-national-duty-speech-text.
4. Rachel Carson, *Silent Spring* (New York: Houghton Mifflin, 1962), pp. 2–3.
5. "American Sewage System and the Price of Optimism," *Time*, August 1, 1969, content.time.com/time/subscriber/article/0,33009,901182-1,00.html.

CHAPTER 2: Spacious Skies and Shining Seas

1. "Current State of the Ozone Layer," US Environmental Protection Agency, www.epa.gov/ozone-layer-protection/current-state-ozone-layer (accessed February 8 2019).
2. "Clean Air Act," USLegal.com, environmentallaw.uslegal.com/federal-laws/clean-air-act (accessed February 13, 2019).
3. Julie Grant, "How a Burning River Helped Create the Clean Water Act," *Allegheny Front*, April 21, 2017, www.alleghenyfront.org/how-a-burning-river-helped-create-the-clean-water-act.

4. Federal Water Pollution Control Act, US Congress, www.epa.gov/sites/production/files/2017-08/documents/federal-water-pollution-control-act-508full.pdf.

5. Richard M. Nixon, First State of the Union, January 22, 1970, www.presidency.ucsb.edu/documents/annual-message-the-congress-the-state-the-union-2.

CHAPTER 3: What Shall We Do with All This Poison?

1. David Germain, "There's No Love Lost for Entrepreneur Who Envisioned Model City," *Los Angeles Times*, May 16, 1993, articles.latimes.com/1993-05-16/news/mn-35999_1_love-canal.

2. Michael H. Brown, "Love Canal and the Poisoning of America," *Atlantic*, December 1979, www.theatlantic.com/magazine/archive/1979/12/love-canal-and-the-poisoning-of-america/376297.

3. Eckardt C. Beck, "The Love Canal Tragedy," *EPA Journal*, January 1979, archive.epa.gov/epa/aboutepa/love-canal-tragedy.html.

4. "Reducing Environmental Cancer Risk: What We Can Do Now," 2008–2009 Annual Report of the President's Cancer Panel, p. 20, deainfo.nci.nih.gov/advisory/pcp/annualReports/pcp08-09rpt/PCP_Report_08-09_508.pdf.

5. "Reducing Environmental Cancer Risk: What We Can Do Now," p. 20.

CHAPTER 4: Where Man Is a Visitor

1. Aldo Leopold, *Sand County Almanac* (New York: Ballantine, 1966), pp. xviii–xix.

2. Max Greenberg, "A Tribute to Howard Zahniser: Unsung Architect of the Wilderness Act," Wilderness Society, February 25, 2016, www.wilderness.org/articles/blog/tribute-howard-zahniser-unsung-architect-wilderness-act.

3. The Wilderness Act of 1964, 16 U.S.C. 1131-1136, wilderness.net/NWPS/documents/publiclaws/PDF/16_USC_1131-1136.pdf.

4. Lyndon B. Johnson, US Forest Service, www.fs.fed.us/managing-land/wilderness.

5. Brian Clark Howard, "Why Federal Lands Are So Wildly Controversial in the West," *National Geographic*, January 4, 2016, news.nationalgeographic.com/2016/01/160104-oregon-protest-malheur-national-wildlife-refuge.

6. Gerardo Ceballos et al., "Accelerated Modern Human-Induced Species Losses: Entering the Sixth Mass Extinction," *Science Advances*, June 19, 2015, advances.sciencemag.org/content/1/5/e1400253.

7. "Extinction Over Time," National Museum of Natural History, naturalhistory.si.edu/education/teaching-resources/paleontology/extinction-over-time (accessed March 8, 2019).

8. Ceballos et al., "Accelerated Modern Human-Induced Species Losses: Entering the Sixth Mass Extinction."

9. Claire Andre and Manuel Velasquez, "The Spotted Owl Controversy," Markkula Ethics Center, Santa Clara University, November 13, 2015, www.scu.edu/environmental-ethics/resources/ethics-and-the-environment-the-spotted-owl.

CHAPTER 5: It's Getting Hot in Here

1. "How Climate Is Changing," NASA, Global Climate Change: Vital Signs of the Planet, climate.nasa.gov/effects (accessed March 7, 2019).

2. "Report on Effects of a Changing Climate to the Department of Defense," United States Department of Defense, January 2019, p. 2, climateandsecurityorg/2019/01/18/new-pentagon-report-the-effects-of-a-changing-climate-are-a-national-security-issue.

3. Richard Conniff, "The Political History of Cap and Trade," *Smithsonian*, August 2009, www.smithsonianmag.com/science-nature/the-political-history-of-cap-and-trade-34711212.

4. Cheryl Hogue, "Greenhouse Gas Emissions Curb: Senators Launch Legislative Effort for US Cap and Trade System," *Chemical and Engineering News*, January 13, 2003, pubs.acs.org/cen/topstory/8102/8102notw1.html.

5. "Adoption of the Paris Agreement," United Nations Framework Convention on Climate Change, November 30 to December 11, 2015, parisclimatetreaty.org/wp-content/uploads/2017/11/EHOTA_Paris_agreement_BOOK.pdf.

CHAPTER 6: Two Steps Forward, One Step Back

1. "Ronald Reagan for President 1980 Campaign Brochure: 'Let's Make America Great Again,'" 4President.org, www.4president.org/brochures/reagan1980brochure1.htm (accessed March 15, 2019).

2. Maggie Koerth-Baker, "A Weaker EPA May Not Mean the Environment Goes to Hell," *FiveThirtyEight*, April 4, 2017, fivethirtyeight.com/features/a-weaker-epa-may-not-mean-the-environment-goes-to-hell.

3. Brady Dennis and Chris Mooney, "Neil Gorsuch's Mother Once Ran the EPA. It Didn't Go Well," *Washington Post*, February 1, 2017, www.washingtonpost.com/news/energy-environment/wp/2017/02/01/neil-gorsuchs-mother-once-ran-the-epa-it-was-a-disaster/?utm_term=.8bd1c0b2a626.

4. Dennis and Mooney, "Neil Gorsuch's Mother Once Ran the EPA. It Didn't Go Well."

5. Frank Newport, "Americans Want Government to Do More on Environment," Gallup, March 29, 2018, news.gallup.com/poll/232007/americans-want-government-more-environment.aspx.

6. Kristen Bialik, "Most Americans Favor Stricter Environmental Laws and Regulations," Pew Research Center, December 14, 2016, www.pewresearch.org/fact-tank/2016/12/14/most-americans-favor-stricter-environmental-laws-and-regulations.

7. "Julianna versus the United States: Youth Climate Lawsuit," Our Children's Trust, www.ourchildrenstrust.org/juliana-v-us (accessed March 18, 2019).

8. John D. Dingell, "My Last Words for America," *Washington Post*, February 8, 2019. www.washingtonpost.com/opinions/john-dingell-my-last-words-for-america/2019/02/08/99220186-2bd3-11e9-984d-9b8fba003e81_story.html?utm_term=.b3c837fcaf9b.

GLOSSARY

act A law or statute passed by a legislative body.

biodiversity The variety of life-forms on Earth, or within a particular ecosystem.

conservation The practice of preserving and protecting wildlife and the natural environment.

dissipate To scatter or thin out, and gradually disappear.

egregious So bad as to be shocking.

emissions Substances that are discharged into the air, such as from factories or automobiles.

fable A short story that conveys a moral or lesson.

fauna Animals.

flora Plants.

glacier A mass of ice, formed in the mountains near the poles, that slowly moves southward.

global warming A gradual trend of increasing average global temperatures.

greenhouse gas A gas, such as carbon dioxide or methane, that absorbs infrared radiation and traps heat in the atmosphere.

incontrovertible Incapable of being denied or disproven.

liability Legal responsibility.

urbanization The increase in the number of cities and number of people who live in cities.

BOOKS

Fabiny, Sarah. *Who Was Rachel Carson?* New York, NY: Penguin Workshop, 2014.

Ignotofsky, Rachel. *The Wondrous Workings of Planet Earth: Understanding Our World and Its Ecosystems*. New York, NY: Ten Speed Press, 2018.

Schwartz, Heather E. *Theodore Roosevelt's Presidency*. Minneapolis, MN: Lerner, 2017.

WEBSITES

Donora Historical Society and Smog Museum
donorahistoricalsociety.org
This website features a detailed history of the Donora smog crisis and includes some contemporary news broadcasts about the event.

Earth Week 1970 (April 16-22)
earthweek1970.org
This website contains a history of the first US Earth Day.

Global Climate Change: Vital Signs of the Planet
climate.nasa.gov
NASA posts continual updates of global average temperature, sea levels, arctic ice, carbon dioxide levels, and other indicators of climate change.

INDEX